Maharshi Dayanand Saraswati Book Series-30

Śri Śaṅkarāchārya's

Ātma-Bodha

Self-Realization

Prof. Ravi Prakash Arya

Chair Professor

Maharshi Dayanand Saraswati Chair (UGC)

Maharshi Dayanand University, Haryana

Assisted by

Alois Heinrich

Amazon Books, USA

In Association with

Indian Foundation for Vedic Science

H.O.1051, Sector-1, Rohtak, Haryana, India

Ph. 9313033917; 9650183260

Email: vedicscience@rediffmail.com; vedicscience@gmail.com

https://vedic-sciences.com

First Edition

Kali Era 5127 (Christian era 2025)

Kalpa Era 1,972,949, 127

Brahma Era 155,521,972,949,127

ISBN: 978-93-94724-29-7

Printed by

Indian Foundation for Vedic Science, 1051, Sector-1, Rohtak-124001, Haryana.

Preface

The Ātma Bodha, as its name suggests, presents a straightforward approach to self-realization. The book's authorship is attributed to Ādi Śaṅkarāchārya. However, a comparison of the Sanskrit of Prasthāna Trayī with the Ātma Bodha reveals no evidence that this concise treatise was also authored by Ādi Śaṅkarāchārya. It must have been written by some later Śaṅkarāchārya. The book comprises 68 verses that address the identities of individuals who can attain self-realization. Overall, the book is quite engaging and elucidates numerous concepts of Vedantic philosophy in accessible terms. Each verse is self-explanatory, eliminating the need for additional explanations that could potentially burden the readers. Regardless of the author's identity, it is evident that an effort has been made to clarify the terms by employing similes. The present translator has made a humble attempt to assign the intended significance to these similes, which are often misunderstood by many authors. The author hopes that readers will find this book to be quite engaging.

Prof. Ravi Prakash Arya

आत्मबोधः

Ātma-Bodhaḥ

Qualified Student

तपोभिः क्षीणपापानां शान्तानां वीतरागिणाम्।
मुमुक्षूणामपेक्ष्योऽयमात्मबोधो विधीयते।।1।।
Tapobhiḥ kṣīṇapāpānāṃ śāntānāṃ vītarāgiṇām.
Mumukṣūṇāmapekṣyo'yamātmabodho vidhīyate //1//

1. Thc Ātma-Bodha (Self-Realization) is composed for those who have destroyed their pāpas (sanskāras responsible for downgradation of human beings to the lower species) through rigorous austerities, maintaining peace and calm demeanor, free from cravings and yearning for liberation.

Self-Knowledge

बोधोऽन्यसाधनेभ्यो हि साक्षान्मोक्षैकसाधनम्।
पाकस्य वह्निवज्ज्ञानं विना मोक्षो न सिध्यति।।2।।
Bodho'nyasādhanebhyo hi sākṣānmokṣaikasādhanam.
Pākasya vahnivajjñānaṃ vinā mokṣo na sidhyati //2//

2. As fire serves as the direct cause of cooking, so too does Self-realization serve as the direct means for emancipation. Unlike other forms of discipline, Self-realization stands alone as the unwavering path to liberation.

अविरोधितया कर्म नाविद्यां विनिवर्तयेत्।
विद्याविद्यां निहन्त्येव तेजस्तिमिरसंघवत्।।3।।
Avirodhitayā karma nāvidyāṃ vinivartayet.
Vidyāvidyāṃ nihantyeva tejastimirasaṃghavat //3//

3. Action cannot remove avidyā (soul's identifying itself with body), as it is not in conflict with or opposed to avidyā (soul's identifying itself with body). Self-

realization, on the other hand, can indeed destroy the soul's identity with the body, akin to light destroying darkness.

Note: Here avidyā means the identification of the soul with the body, and vidya means identifying one's true nature.

अवच्छिन्न इवाज्ञानात्तन्नाशे सति केवलः ।
स्वयं प्रकाशते ह्यात्मा मेघापायेंऽशुमानिव ।।4।।
Avacchinna ivājñānāttannāśe sati kevalaḥ.
Svayaṃ prakāśate hyātmā meghāpāyeṃ'śumāniva //4//

4. The soul appears concealed [ajñānāt] due to its identification with the body. When the soul's identification with the body is eliminated, the soul alone radiates, akin to the sun when the clouds are dispersed.

अज्ञानकलुषं जीवं ज्ञानाभ्यासाद्विनिर्मलम् ।
कृत्वा ज्ञानं स्वयं नश्येज्जलं कतकरेणुवत् ।।5।।
Ajñānakaluṣaṃ jīvaṃ jñānābhyāsādvinirmalam.
Kṛtvā jñānaṃ svayaṃ naśyejjalaṃ katakareṇuvat //5//

5. The [jīvam] embodied soul, stained by its identification with the body, is cleansed by constant practice of self-realization. When self–realization occurs soul's identification with the body is destroyed, as the powder of the Kataka (clearing-nut) settles down after it has cleansed the muddy water.

संसारः स्वप्नतुल्यो हि रागद्वेषादिसंकुलः ।
स्वकाले सत्यवद्भाति प्रबोधे सत्यसद्भवेत् ।।6।।
Saṃsāraḥ svapnatulyo hi rāgadveṣādisaṃkulaḥ.
Svakāle satyavadbhāti prabodhe satyasadbhavet //6//

6. The world of living beings, characterized by the coexistence of love and hatred, is akin to a dream. While it appears tangible during its duration, it becomes illusory upon awakening to one's true nature.

तावत्सत्यं जगद्भाति शुक्तिकारजतं यथा।
यावन्न ज्ञायते ब्रह्म सर्वाधिष्ठानमद्वयम्।।7।।
Tāvatsatyaṃ jagadbhāti śuktikārajataṃ yathā.
Yāvanna jñāyate brahma sarvādhiṣṭhānamadvayam ।।7।।

7. The Jagat (world in motion) appears to be eternal, so long as Brahman, the efficient cause of the entire creation and who has no parallel, is not realised. It is like the appearance of silver in the oyster-shell, so long as the oyster-shell is not truly identified.

उपादानेऽखिलाधारे जगन्ति परमेश्वरे।
सर्गस्थितिलयान्यान्ति बुद्बुदानीव वारिणि।।8।।
Upādāne'khilādhāre jaganti parameśvare.
Sargasthitilayānyānti budbudānīva vāriṇi ।।8।।

8. Like bubbles in water, the worlds rise, exist, and dissolve in the material cause (prakṛti), governed by Brahman.

Note: Here, the words upādāna and Parameśvara are not used as qualifiers and qualified, rather as two distinct nouns. Upādāna is used to denote Prakṛti, which is governed by Parameśvara.

सच्चिदात्मन्यनुस्यूते नित्ये विष्णौ प्रकल्पिताः।
व्यक्तयो विविधाः सर्वा हाटके कटकादिवत्।।9।।
Saccidātmanyanusyūte nitye viṣṇau prakalpitāḥ.
Vyaktayo vividhāḥ sarvā hāṭake kaṭakādivat ।।9।।

9. Various individual creations are pervaded by eternal, all-pervading, sachchitātma Brahman, just as the different ornaments of gold are pervaded by Gold.

यथाकाशो हृषीकेशो नानोपाधिगतो विभुः।
तद्भेदाद्भिन्नवद्भाति तन्नाशे केवलो भवेत्।।10।।
Yathākāśo hṛṣīkeśo nānopādhigato vibhuḥ.
Tadbhedādbhinnavadbhāti tannāśe kevalo bhavet ।।10।।

10. Just as the all-pervading space appears diverse due

to diverse upādhis (separating boundaries such as walls of rooms, etc.), it becomes unified when those boundaries are dismantled. Similarly, Brahman appears diverse due to diverse [upādhis] qualities. When one understands that these different qualities belong to one and the same Brahman, it does not appear diverse.

नानोपाधिवशादेव जातिनामाश्रमादयः ।
आत्मन्यारोपितास्तोये रसवर्णादिभेदवत् । ।11 । ।
nānopādhivaśādeva jātināmāśramādayaḥ.
ātmanyāropitāstoye rasavarṇādibhedavat / /11 / /

11. Similarly, due to various upādhis of bodies, souls are [āropitāḥ] placed in various species and āśramas, just as waters have various flavors and colors due to the association of various upādhis (of colors and flavors).

पञ्चीकृतमहाभूतसंभवं कर्मसंचितम् ।
शरीरं सुखदुःखानां भोगायतनमुच्यते । ।12 । ।
Pañcīkṛtamahābhūtasaṃbhavaṃ karmasaṃcitam.
Śarīraṃ sukhaduḥkhānāṃ bhogāyatanamucyate / /12 / /

12. The bodies of souls are determined by their accumulated past karmas. This process of formation of bodies involves the combination of five elements through a process called pañchīkaraṇa (permutation and combination of five bhūtas). The body serves as the medium through which individuals experience both pleasure and pain.

पञ्चप्राणमनोबुद्धिदशेन्द्रियसमन्वितम् ।
अपञ्चीकृतभूतोत्थं सूक्ष्माङ्गं भोगसाधनम् । ।13 । ।
Pañcaprāṇamanobuddhidaśendriyasamanvitam.
Apañcīkṛtabhūtotthaṃ sūkṣmāṅgaṃ
bhogasādhanam / /13 / /

13. The body, a combination of the five prāṇas (apāna, vyāna, prāṇa, udāna, samāna), ten organs (five senses and

five motor organs), manas (mind), and buddhi, formed from subtle elements (tanmātras) that haven't undergone the process of pañchikaraṇa, serves as the means for the experience of the soul.

अनाद्यविद्यानिर्वाच्या कारणोपाधिरुच्यते ।
उपाधित्रितयादन्यमात्मानमवधारयेत् । ।14 । ।
Anādyavidyānirvācyā kāraṇopādhirucyate.
Upādhitritayādanyamātmānamavadhārayet । ।14 । ।

14. [Avidyā] The soul's identification with the body is an eternal and indescribable (natural) process. The sanskāra of avidyā is the cause of the soul's embodiment (bondage). It is crucial to recognize that the Ātman is distinct from the three Upādhis: mind, buddhi and the body.

पञ्चकोशादियोगेन तत्तन्मय इव स्थितः ।
शुद्धात्मा नीलवस्त्रादियोगेन स्फटिको यथा । ।15 । ।
Pañcakośādiyogena tattanmaya iva sthitaḥ.
Śuddhātmā nīlavastrādiyogena sphaṭiko yathā । ।15 । ।

15. Due to its conjunction with five koṣas, the soul appears to be like them; just as a crystal appears to be of the same color to which it is conjuncted.

Note: Bodies in five koṣas are illustrated below:

1. Annamaya koṣa: Plants, trees, shrubs and herbs.
2. Prāṇamaya koṣa: Small insects, bacterias etc.
3. Manomaya koṣa: Animals and birds.
4. Vijñānamaya koṣa: Human beings.
5. Ānandamaya koṣa: Divine beings.

वपुस्तुषादिभिः कोशैर्युक्तं युक्त्यवघाततः ।
आत्मानमान्तरं शुद्धं विविञ्च्यात्तण्डुलं यथा । ।16 । ।
Vapustuṣādibhiḥ kośairyuktaṃ yuktyavaghātataḥ.
Ātmānamāntaraṃ śuddhaṃ viviñcyāttaṇḍulaṃ yathā । ।16 । ।

16. [yuktyā] Through logical thinking, one should [vivichyāt] discriminate the [śuddhaṁ] pure [ātmānam] self, which is [yuktam] covered [āntaram] within the [vapuḥ] bodies of [kośaiḥ] five koṣas, just as one separates [taṇḍlam] the rice covered [tuṣādibhiḥ] under the husk by [avaghātataḥ] pounding it.

सदा सर्वगतोऽप्यात्मा न सर्वत्रावभासते ।
बुद्धावेवावभासेत स्वच्छेषु प्रतिबिम्बवत् । ।17 । ।
Sadā sarvagato'pyātmā na sarvatrāvabhāsate.
Buddhāvevāvabhāseta svaccheṣu pratibimbavat । ।17 । ।

17. The Brahman, though all-pervading, cannot be seen by everybody. His presence is discernible to the mind purified through yoga, just as an object's [pratibimba] reflection is obtained in a [svacheṣu] clean mirror.

देहेन्द्रियमनोबुद्धिप्रकृतिभ्यो विलक्षणम् ।
तद्वृत्तिसाक्षिणं विद्यादात्मानं राजवत्सदा । ।18 । ।
Dehendriyamanobuddhiprakṛtibhyo vilakṣaṇam.
Tadvṛttisākṣiṇaṃ vidyādātmānaṃ rājavatsadā । ।18 । ।

18. One should understand that the Ātman is distinct from the body, senses, mind, and intellect, all of which are composed of matter (Prakṛti). The Ātman serves as the witness of their functions, similar to how a king observes the activities of people.

व्यापृतेष्विन्द्रियेष्वात्मा व्यापारीवाविवेकिनाम् ।
दृश्यतेऽभ्रेषु धावत्सु धावन्निव यथा शशी । ।19 । ।
Vyāpṛteṣvindriyeṣvātmā vyāpārīvāvivekinām.
Dṛśyate'bhreṣu dhāvatsu dhāvanniva yathā śaśī । ।19 । ।

19. When the body, mind, and sense organs function, unwise individuals mistakenly believe that the Ātman is actively engaged, just as the moon appears to be moving when the clouds in the sky shift.

आत्मचैतन्यमाश्रित्य देहेन्द्रियमनोधियः ।

स्वकीयार्थेषु वर्तन्ते सूर्यालोकं यथा जनाः ।।20।।
Ātmacaitanyamāśritya dehendriyamanodhiyaḥ.
Svakīyārtheṣu vartante sūryālokaṃ yathā janāḥ ।।20।।

20. The body, senses, mind, and buddhi engage in their respective activities with the assistance of the spiritual element, Ātman, just as humans work with the aid of the Sun's light.

देहेन्द्रियगुणान्कर्माण्यमले सच्चिदात्मनि ।
अध्यस्यन्त्यविवेकेन गगने नीलतादिवत् ।।21।।
Dehendriyaguṇānkarmāṇyamale saccidātmani.
Adhyasyantyavivekena gagane nīlatādivat ।।21।।

21. People, due to ignorance, mistakenly attribute the qualities and functions of the body and senses to the Ātman, just as they mistakenly attribute blue color and the like to the sky.

अज्ञानान्मानसोपाधेः कर्तृत्वादीनि चात्मनि ।
कल्प्यन्तेऽम्बुगते चन्द्रे चलनादि यथाम्भसः ।।22।।
Ajñānānmānasopādheḥ kartṛtvādīni cātmani.
Kalpyante'mbugate candre calanādi yathāmbhasaḥ ।।22।।

22. The functions of the mind, which is the delimiting factor of the Ātman, are mistakenly attributed to the Ātman itself, just as tremblings of the moon in the waters are mistakenly attributed to the moon reflected in them.

रागेच्छासुखदुःखादि बुद्धौ सत्यां प्रवर्तते ।
सुषुप्तौ नास्ति तन्नाशे तस्माद्बुद्धेस्तु नात्मनः ।।23।।
Rāgecchāsukhaduḥkhādi buddhau satyāṃ pravartate.
Suṣuptau nāsti tannāśe tasmādbuddhestu nātmanaḥ ।।23।।

23. Attachment, desire, pleasure, pain, and so on, are perceived to exist as long as [buddhau] the mind functions. They are not perceived during deep sleep when the mind ceases to function. Hence, they belong solely to the mind and not to the Ātman.

प्रकाशोऽर्कस्य तोयस्य शैत्यमग्नेर्यथोष्णता।
स्वभावः सच्चिदानन्दनित्यनिर्मलतात्मनः।।24।।
Prakāśo'rkasya toyasya śaityamagneryathoṣṇatā.
Svabhāvaḥ saccidānandanityanirmalatātmanaḥ ।।24।।

24. Just as the Sun embodies luminosity, water coolness, and fire heat, so too does the Ātman embody eternity, purity, reality, knowledge, and bliss.

आत्मनः सच्चिदंशश्च बुद्धेर्वृत्तिरिति द्वयम्।
संयोज्य चाविवेकेन जानामीति प्रवर्तते।।25।।
Ātmanaḥ saccidaṃśaśca buddhervṛttiriti dvayam.
Saṃyojya cāvivekena jānāmīti pravartate ।।25।।

25. When the existential and knowledge aspects of the soul are integrated with the functions of the mind, the notion of "I know" emerges due to inability to distinguish between the functions of soul and mind.

आत्मनो विक्रिया नास्ति बुद्धेर्बोधो न जात्विति।
जीवः सर्वमलं ज्ञात्वा ज्ञाता द्रष्टेति मुह्यति।।26।।
Ātmano vikriyā nāsti buddherbodho na jātviti.
Jīvaḥ sarvamalaṃ jñātvā jñātā draṣṭeti muhyati ।।26।।

26. The ātman lacks the power to act, and buddhi lacks the power to comprehend on its own. However, the embodied soul mistakenly believes that it is the seer and the knower alone.

रज्जुसर्पवदात्मानं जीवं ज्ञात्वा भयं वहेत्।
नाहं जीवः परात्मेति ज्ञातश्चेन्निर्भयो भवेत्।।27।।
Rajjusarpavadātmānaṃ jīvaṃ jñātvā bhayaṃ vahet.
Nāhaṃ jīvaḥ parātmeti jñātaścennirbhayo bhavet ।।27।।

27. Just as a person who perceives a rope as a snake is overcome by fear, so too is one who considers their body as the soul overcome by fear. By realizing that they are not an embodied soul but the pure Soul itself, which is beyond body, one can attain fearlessness.

आत्मावभासयत्येको बुद्ध्यादीनीन्द्रियाणि हि।
दीपो घटादिवत्स्वात्मा जडैस्तैर्नावभास्यते।।28।।
Ātmāvabhāsayatyeko buddhyādīnīndriyāṇi hi.
Dīpo ghaṭādivatsvātmā jaḍaistairnāvabhāsyate ।।28।।

28. Similarly, as a lamp illuminates a jar or a pot, so too does the Ātman illuminate the mind and the sense organs, and so on. These material objects, in their own right, cannot illuminate themselves because they are inert.

स्वबोधे नान्यबोधेच्छा बोधरूपतयात्मनः।
न दीपस्यान्यदीपेच्छा यथा स्वात्मप्रकाशने।।29।।
Svabodhe nānyabodhecchā bodharūpatayātmanaḥ.
Na dīpasyānyadīpecchā yathā svātmaprakāśane ।।29।।

29. A lighted lamp does not require another lamp to illuminate it. Similarly, the Ātman, which is of the nature of knowledge itself, does not necessitate the knowledge of other for its self-realisation.

निषिध्य निखिलोपाधीन्नेति नेतीति वाक्यतः।
विद्यादैक्यं महावाक्यैर्जीवात्मपरमात्मनोः।।30।।
Niṣidhya nikhilopādhīnneti netīti vākyataḥ.
Vidyādaikyaṃ mahāvākyairjīvātmaparamātmanoḥ ।।30।।

30. By systematically ruling out the Upādhis (such as the body, sense organs, mind, buddhi, and so on) through the use of statements like "It is not this" and "It is not that," the profound realization of the unity of the embodied soul and the soul beyond the body (pure soul), as elucidated in the esteemed Mahāvākyas, becomes attainable.

Note: Here embodied soul is jīvātmā and pure soul (soul wihout body) is addressed as paramātman,

आविद्यकं शरीरादि दृश्यं बुद्बुदवत्क्षरम्।
एतद्विलक्षणं विद्यादहं ब्रह्मेति निर्मलम्।।31।।
Āvidyakaṃ śarīrādi dṛśyaṃ budbudavatkṣaram.

Etadvilakṣaṇaṃ vidyādahaṃ brahmeti nirmalam । ।31 । ।

31. From the causal body (sanskāras of the material world) to the visible physical body, all are impermanent and akin to bubbles. Recognize that the pure Ātman is fundamentally distinct from them and is referred to as 'Aham' in technical terms of philosophy.

Note: In Vedānta, it is repeatedly told that the personal pronouns I, my, and me are terms typically used to refer to Ātman or Parmātman, but many people mistakenly believe these pronouns are applicable to human beings. A clear example of this confusion can be found in the Bhagavad Gītā. In the Gītā, the words "Aham" and "mama" are used to refer to God, yet those who are not well-informed often apply them to Śri Krishna.

देहान्यत्वान्न मे जन्मजराकार्श्यलयादयः ।
शब्दादिविषयैः सङ्गो निरिन्द्रियतया न च । ।32 । ।
Dehānyatvānna me janmajarākārśyalayādayaḥ.
Śabdādiviṣayaiḥ saṅgo nirindriyatayā na ca । ।32 । ।

32. The soul, distinct from the body, is impervious to alterations such as birth, aging, wrinkling, senility, and death. It is not associated with sensory experiences like sound and taste, as the soul lacks the corresponding sense organs.

Note: Here 'soul' is addressed by the first person pronoun.

अमनस्त्वान्न मे दुःखरागद्वेषभयादयः ।
अप्राणो ह्यमनाः शुभ्र इत्यादिश्रुतिशासनात् । ।33 । ।
Amanastvānna me duḥkharāgadveṣabhayādayaḥ.
Aprāṇo hyamanāḥ śubhra ityādiśrutiśāsanāt । ।33 । ।

33. The soul, distinct from the mind, is liberated from sorrow, attachment, malice, and fear, as the scriptures describe it as breathless, mindless, pure, and identical.

निर्गुणो निष्क्रियो नित्यो निर्विकल्पो निरञ्जनः ।
निर्विकारो निराकारो नित्यमुक्तोऽस्मि निर्मलः । ।34 । ।
Nirguṇo niṣkriyo nityo nirvikalpo nirañjanaḥ.
Nirvikāro nirākāro nityamukto'smi nirmalaḥ । ।34 । ।

34. The Brahman is devoid of attributes, motion, desires, thoughts, dirt, change, form, and liberation. It is ever-liberated and ever-pure.

अहमाकाशवत्सर्वं बहिरन्तर्गतोऽच्युतः ।
सदा सर्वसमः सिद्धो निःसङ्गो निर्मलोऽचलः । ।35 । ।
Ahamākāśavatsarvaṃ bahirantargato'cyutaḥ.
Sadā sarvasamaḥ siddho niḥsaṅgo nirmalo'calaḥ । ।35 । ।

35. Similarly to the vastness of space, Brahman permeates all aspects of existence, both within and without. Brahman remains unchanging and consistent, embodying purity, immaturity, unattachment, immaculacy, and tranquility.

Note: Here Brahman is addressed by the term 'Aham'.

नित्यशुद्धविमुक्तैकमखण्डानन्दमद्वयम् ।
सत्यं ज्ञानमनन्तं यत्परं ब्रह्माहमेव तत् । ।36 । ।
Nityaśuddhavimuktaikamakhaṇḍānandamadvayam.
Satyaṃ jñānamanantaṃ yatparaṃ brahmāhameva tat । ।36 । ।

36. Brahman known as 'Aham' is Eternal, Pure and Free, One, Indivisible, Non-dual, Changeless, All-knowledge and Infinite.

एवं निरन्तरकृता ब्रह्मैवास्मीति वासना ।
हरत्यविद्याविक्षेपान्रोगानिव रसायनम् । ।37 । ।
Evaṃ nirantarakṛtā brahmaivāsmīti vāsanā.
Haratyavidyāvikṣepānrogāniva rasāyanam । ।37 । ।

37. The consistent practice of yoga helps in realization that "I am the soul (not the body)," which effectively destroys avidyā (the mistaken belief that the soul is the

body) and the distractions it causes, just as Rasāyana destroys diseases.

विविक्तदेश आसीनो विरागो विजितेन्द्रियः।
भावयेदेकमात्मानं तमनन्तमनन्यधीः।।38।।
Viviktadeśa āsīno virāgo vijitendriyaḥ.
Bhāvayedekamātmānaṃ tamanantamananyadhīḥ।।*38*।।

38. In solitude, free the mind from desires and controlling the senses, meditate with unwavering attention on the Brahman, the One without a second.

आत्मन्येवाखिलं दृश्यं प्रविलाप्य धिया सुधीः।
भावयेदेकमात्मानं निर्मलाकाशवत्सदा।।39।।
Ātmanyevākhilaṃ dṛśyaṃ pravilāpya dhiyā sudhīḥ.
Bhāvayedekamātmānaṃ nirmalākāśavatsadā।।*39*।।

39. The enlightened individual should skillfully integrate the entire visible realm into Brahman alone and perpetually meditate upon Brahman, recognizing that it is perpetually not tainted by impurities, akin to the sky.

रूपवर्णादिकं सर्वं विहाय परमार्थवित्।
परिपूर्णचिदानन्दस्वरूपेणावतिष्ठते।।40।।
Rūpavarṇādikaṃ sarvaṃ vihāya paramārthavit.
Paripūrṇacidānandasvarūpeṇāvatiṣṭhate।।*40*।।

40. He who has realized the Supreme Brahman renounces all identification with the objects of names and forms. Afterward, he dwells with Brahman, who is complete and blissful.

ज्ञातृज्ञानज्ञेयभेदः परे नात्मनि विद्यते।
चिदानन्दैकरूपत्वाद्दीप्यते स्वयमेव हि।।41।।
Jñātṛjñānajñeyabhedaḥ pare nātmani vidyate.
Cidānandaikarūpatvāddīpyate svayameva hi।।*41*।।

41. There are no distinctions such as "Knower," "Knowledge," and "Object of Knowledge" in the Mokṣa (Supreme Self). Due to its nature of endless bliss, the

Brahman alone shines by itself (in Mokṣa).

एवमात्मारणौ ध्यानमथने सततं कृते ।
उदितावगतिज्वाला सर्वाज्ञानेन्धनं दहेत् । ।42 । ।
Evamātmāraṇau dhyānamathane satataṃ kṛte.
Uditāvagatijvālā sarvājñānendhanaṃ dahet । ।42 । ।

42. Through the relentless churning of meditation on Brahman, akin to the attrition of wood used for kindling fire, the fire of knowledge thus grown shall ignite and consume all the fuel of ignorance within us.

अरुणेनेव बोधेन पूर्वं संतमसे हृते ।
तत आविर्भवेदात्मा स्वयमेवांशुमानिव । ।43 । ।
Aruṇeneva bodhena pūrvaṃ saṃtamase hṛte.
Tata āvirbhavedātmā svayamevāṃśumāniva । ।43 । ।

43. The illumination of self-realization has already dispelled the profound darkness of avidyā. Subsequently, the soul ascends alone, akin to the self-effulgent sun.

आत्मा तु सततं प्राप्तोऽप्यप्राप्तवदविद्यया ।
तन्नाशे प्राप्तवद्भाति स्वकण्ठाभरणं यथा । ।44 । ।
Ātmā tu satataṃ prāpto'pyaprāptavadavidyayā.
Tannāśe prāptavadbhāti svakaṇṭhābharaṇaṃ yathā । ।44 । ।

44. Ātman, an ever-present reality, remains absent due to avidyā. However, upon the destruction of avidyā, Ātman manifests as if present, akin to the missing ornament of one's neck.

स्थाणौ पुरुषवद्भ्रान्त्या कृता ब्रह्मणि जीवता ।
जीवस्य तात्त्विके रूपे तस्मिन्दृष्टे निवर्तते । ।45 । ।
Sthāṇau puruṣavadbhrāntyā kṛtā brahmaṇi jīvatā.
Jīvasya tāttvike rūpe tasmindṛṣṭe nivartate । ।45 । ।

45. The soul gets embodied because of the confusion of identifying itself with the body, just as a post appears to be a human figure. When the true nature of the embodied soul is realized, the entire confusion is resolved.

तत्त्वस्वरूपानुभवादुत्पन्नं ज्ञानमञ्जसा।
अहं ममेति चाज्ञानं बाधते दिग्भ्रमादिवत्।।46।।
Tattvasvarūpānubhavādutpannaṃ jñānamañjasā.
Ahaṃ mameti cājñānaṃ bādhate digbhramādivat I I46 I I

46. When the true nature of the soul is realized, the knowledge of its true nature effectively destroys the erroneous concept of 'I' and 'Mine', just as accurate information eliminates the incorrect notion about directions.

सम्यग्विज्ञानवान्योगी स्वात्मन्येवाखिलं स्थितम्।
एकं च सर्वमात्मानमीक्षते ज्ञानचक्षुषा।।47।।
Samyagvijñānavānyogī svātmanyevākhilaṃ sthitam.
Ekaṃ ca sarvamātmānamīkṣate jñānacakṣuṣā I I47 I I

47. The Yogi of true realization perceives the entire universe within himself, viewing all living beings akin to himself.

आत्मैवेदं जगत्सर्वमात्मनोऽन्यन्न किंचन।
मृदो यद्वद्धटादीनि स्वात्मानं सर्वमीक्षते।।48।।
Ātmaivedaṃ jagatsarvamātmano'nyanna kiṃcana.
Mṛdo yadvaddhaṭādīni svātmānaṃ sarvamīkṣate I I48 I I

48. Nothing whatsoever exists as a living being except the Ātman, as all living beings have the essence of souls. Just as pots and jars are indeed made of clay and cannot be mistaken for anything else, the enlightened soul perceives every living being as like itself.

जीवन्मुक्तस्तु तद्विद्वान्पूर्वोपाधिगुणांस्त्यजेत्।
स सच्चिदादिधर्मत्वं भेजे भ्रमरकीटवत्।।49।।
Jīvanmuktastu tadvidvānpūrvopādhiguṇāṃstyajet.
Sa saccidādidharmatvaṃ bheje bhramarakīṭavat I I49 I I

49. A liberated being is one who sheds the traits inherited from its previous body and embraces its true nature of [sat] eternity [chit] and chetanā (immaterial).

This transformation is akin to a young wasp assuming its authentic nature as it matures.

तीर्त्वा मोहार्णवं हत्वा रागद्वेषादिराक्षसान्।
योगी शान्तिसमायुक्त आत्मा रामो विराजते।।50।।
Tīrtvā mohārṇavaṃ hatvā rāgadveṣādirākṣasān.
Yogī śāntisamāyukta ātmā rāmo virājate / /50 / /

50. After transcending the realm of delusion and vanquishing the monsters of likes and dislikes, the yogi who has attained peace dwells in the radiance of their own realized self. (Ātmārāma).

बाह्यानित्यसुखासक्तिं हित्वात्मसुखनिर्वृतः।
घटस्थदीपवच्छश्वदन्तरेव प्रकाशते।।51।।
Bāhyānityasukhāsaktiṃ hitvātmasukhanirvṛtaḥ.
Ghaṭasthadīpavacchaśvadantareva prakāśate / /51 / /

51. The Living liberated soul, releasing all its attachments to the impermanent external comforts, finds contentment in the bliss derived from the within. This enlightened being radiates inwardly, akin to a lamp placed within a jar.

उपाधिस्थोऽपि तद्धर्मैरलिप्तो व्योमवन्मुनिः।
सर्वविन्मूढवत्तिष्ठेदसक्तो वायुवच्चरेत्।।52।।
Upādhistho'pi taddharmairalipto vyomavanmuniḥ.
Sarvavinmūḍhavattiṣṭhedasakto vāyuvaccaret / /52 / /

52. Although the living liberated soul resides within the physical form, it remains perpetually unaffiliated with its material properties, akin to the space that permeates all entities, yet remains impervious to their influence. Despite possessing complete knowledge, they live in a state of detachment, akin to an innocent individual. They traverse life like the wind, perfectly unattached.

उपाधिविलयाद्विष्णौ निर्विशेषं विशेन्मुनिः।
जले जलं वियद्व्योम्नि तेजस्तेजसि वा यथा।।53।।

Upādhivilayādviṣṇau nirviśeṣaṃ viśenmuniḥ.
Jale jalaṃ viyadvyomni tejastejasi vā yathā | |53 | |

53. Upon the dissolution of the physical form, the seeker achieves a state of profound absorption within the divine essence of Viṣṇu (Brahman), the omnipresent Spirit. This union is akin to the merging of water into water, space into space, and light into light.

यल्लाभान्नापरो लाभो यत्सुखान्नापरं सुखम् ।
यज्ज्ञानान्नापरं ज्ञानं तद्ब्रह्मेत्यवधारयेत् । ।54 । ।
Yallābhānnāparo lābho yatsukhānnāparaṃ sukham.
Yajjñānānnāparaṃ jñānaṃ tadbrahmetyavadhārayet | |54 | |

54. Know that to be Brahman, the attainment of which leaves nothing more to be attained, the bliss of which leaves no other bliss to be sought, and the knowledge of which leaves nothing more to be known.

यद्दृष्ट्वा नापरं दृश्यं यद्भूत्वा न पुनर्भवः ।
यज्ज्ञात्वा नापरं ज्ञेयं तद्ब्रह्मेत्यवधारयेत् । ।55 । ।
Yaddṛṣṭvā nāparaṃ dṛśyaṃ yadbhūtvā na punarbhavaḥ.
Yajjñātvā nāparaṃ jñeyaṃ tadbrahmetyavadhārayet | |55 | |

55. Understand that to be Brahman, the sight of which transcends all perception, merging into which liberates one from the cycle of birth and death, and the knowledge of which reveals nothing more to be discovered.

तिर्यगूर्ध्वमधः पूर्णं सच्चिदानन्दमद्वयम् ।
अनन्तं नित्यमेकं यत्तद्ब्रह्मेत्यवधारयेत् । ।56 । ।
Tiryagūrdhvamadhaḥ pūrṇaṃ saccidānandamadvayam.
Anantaṃ nityamekaṃ yattadbrahmetyavadhārayet | |56 | |

56. Know that to be Brahman which is Truth, Chetana and Bliss, which is unparalleled, Infinite, Eternal, and One, and which fills all the quarters – above and below and across.

अतद्व्यावृत्तिरूपेण वेदान्तैर्लक्ष्यतेऽव्ययम् ।

अखण्डानन्दमेकं यत्तद्ब्रह्मेत्यवधारयेत् । ।57 । ।
Atadvyāvṛttirūpeṇa vedāntairlakṣyate'vyayam.
Akhaṇḍānandamekaṃ yattadbrahmetyavadhārayet । ।57 । ।

57. Know that to be Brahman, which is imperishable, indivisible, blissful, one, and which is indicated [vyāvṛttirupeṇa] through the process of ruling out of tangible objects (like neti, neti) by those who have attained the culmination of knowledge (Vedānta Philosophers).

अखण्डानन्दरूपस्य तस्यानन्दलवाश्रिताः ।
ब्रह्माद्यास्तारतम्येन भवन्त्यानन्दिनोऽखिलाः । ।58 । ।
Akhaṇḍānandarūpasya tasyānandalavāśritāḥ.
Brahmādyāstāratamyena bhavantyānandino'khilāḥ । ।58 । ।

58. Brahmā and others experience only a tiny fraction of the boundless bliss of Brahman, and their enjoyment is proportional to their appreciation of it.

तद्युक्तमखिलं वस्तु व्यवहारश्चिदन्वितः ।
तस्मात्सर्वगतं ब्रह्म क्षीरे सर्पिरिवाखिले । ।59 । ।
Tadyuktamakhilaṃ vastu vyavahāraścidanvitaḥ.
Tasmātsarvagataṃ brahma kṣīre sarpirivākhile । ।59 । ।

59. Brahman permeates everything, just as butter permeates milk. All objects are pervaded by Brahman, and all actions and motions are possible because of Brahman.

अनण्वस्थूलमह्रस्वमदीर्घमजमव्ययम् ।
अरूपगुणवर्णाख्यं तद्ब्रह्मेत्यवधारयेत् । ।60 । ।
Anaṇvasthūlamahrasvamadīrghamajamavyayam.
Arūpaguṇavarṇākhyaṃ tadbrahmetyavadhārayet । ।60 । ।

60. Understand that Brahman is neither subtle nor gross, neither short nor long, without birth or change. It is formless, devoid of qualities and colors.

यद्भासा भास्यतेऽर्कादि भास्यैर्यत्तु न भास्यते ।
येन सर्वमिदं भाति तद्ब्रह्मेत्यवधारयेत् । ।61 । ।

Yadbhāsā bhāsyate'rkādi bhāsyairyattu na bhāsyate.
Yena sarvamidaṃ bhāti tadbrahmetyavadhārayet I I61 I I

61. Understand that Brahman is the light that illuminates the luminous stars, but it is not illuminated by their light. It is the source of all illumination.

स्वयमन्तर्बहिर्व्याप्य भासयन्नखिलं जगत्।
ब्रह्म प्रकाशते वह्निप्रतप्तायसपिण्डवत्।।62।।
Svayamantarbahirvyāpya bhāsayannakhilaṃ jagat.
Brahma prakāśate vahnipratapṭāyasapiṇḍavat I I62 I I

62. The Supreme Brahman permeates the entire universe, both outwardly and inwardly, making the entire world shine. Brahman shines from within, like the fire that permeates a red-hot iron ball and glows independently.

जगद्विलक्षणं ब्रह्म ब्रह्मणोऽन्यन्न किंचन।
ब्रह्मान्यद्भाति चेन्मिथ्या यथा मरुमरीचिका।।63।।
Jagadvilakṣaṇaṃ brahma brahmaṇo'nyanna kiṃcana.
Brahmānyadbhāti cenmithyā yathā marumarīcikā I I63 I I

63. Brahman, the ultimate reality, is distinct from this world. Nothing exists independently of Brahman; everything is pervaded by it. If an object appears to exist separately from Brahman, it is an illuson, like a mirage.

दृश्यते श्रूयते यद्यद्ब्रह्मणोऽन्यन्न तद्भवेत्।
तत्त्वज्ञानाच्च तद्ब्रह्म सच्चिदानन्दमद्वयम्।।64।।
Dṛśyate śrūyate yadyadbrahmaṇo'nyanna tadbhavet.
Tattvajñānācca tadbrahma saccidānandamadvayam I I64 I I

64. Brahman permeates everything perceived or heard, leaving no room for anything else. By attaining knowledge of the Reality, one perceives the Universe as pervaded by the non-dual Brahman, Who is ultimate truth, all knowledge, and all bliss.

सर्वगं सच्चिदानन्दं ज्ञानचक्षुर्निरीक्षते।
अज्ञानचक्षुर्नेक्षेत भास्वन्तं भानुमन्धवत्।।65।।

Sarvagaṃ saccidānandaṃ jñānacakṣurnirīkṣate.
Ajñānacakṣurnekṣeta bhāsvantaṃ bhānumandhavat / /65 / /

65. Brahman, the ever-present, all-knowing, and all-blissful ultimate truth, can only be perceived by the eye of wisdom. However, those whose vision is obscured by ignorance fail to see it, just as the blind cannot see the radiant Sun.

श्रवणादिभिरुद्दीप्त
ज्ञानाग्निपरितापितः ।
जीवः सर्वमलान्मुक्तः
स्वर्णवद्द्योतते स्वयम् । ।66 । ।
Śravaṇādibhiruddīpta
Jñānāgniparitāpitaḥ.
Jīvaḥ sarvamalānmuktaḥ
Svarṇavaddyotate svayam / /66 / /

66. The Jīva, the embodied soul, free from impurities, is illuminated by the fire of knowledge kindled through hearing and other means. It shines by itself like gold.

हृदाकाशोदितो ह्यात्मा
बोधभानुस्तमोपहृत् ।
सर्वव्यापी सर्वधारी
भाति भासयतेऽखिलम् । ।67 । ।
Hṛdākāśodito hyātmā
Bodhabhānustamopahṛt.
Sarvavyāpī sarvadhārī
Bhāti bhāsayate'khilam / /67 / /

67. The Brahman is the Sun of Knowledge that rises in the sky of the heart, dispelling the darkness of ignorance. It permeates and sustains all and shines and makes everything shine.

दिग्देशकालाद्यनपेक्ष्य सर्वगं
शीतादिहृन्नित्यसुखं निरञ्जनम् ।
यः स्वात्मतीर्थं भजते विनिष्क्रियः

स सर्ववित्सर्वगतोऽमृतो भवेत् । ।68 । ।
Digdeśakālādyanapekṣya sarvagaṃ
Śītādihṛnnityasukhaṃ nirañjanam.
Yaḥ svātmatīrthaṃ bhajate viniṣkriyaḥ
Sa sarvavitsarvagato'mṛto bhavet । ।68 । ।

68. He, who renouncing all activities, aproaches his own soul which is akin to a tīrtha, which transcends all the limitations of time, space and direction, which is present everywhere, which is the destroyer of the feeling of heat and cold, which is eternal bliss and stainless, attains Brahman who is all-knowing and all-pervading.

इति श्रीमत्परमहंस परिव्राजकाचार्यस्य श्रीगोविन्दभगव
त्पूज्यपादशिष्यस्य श्रीमच्छंकरभगवतः कृतौआत्मबोधः संपूर्णः । ।
Iti śrīmatparamahaṃsa parivrājakācāryasya
śrīgovindabhagavä
Tpūjyapādaśiṣyasya śrīmacchaṃkarabhagavataḥ kṛtau
Ātmabodhaḥ saṃpūrṇaḥ । ।

Thus is completed Ātmabodha, authored by Śrimat Śaṅkarāchārya, a disciple of Śri Govindāchāarya.